Gift of the
Hackbarth Foundation
2015

AMERICAN SPECIAL OPS

THE U.S. ARMY GREEN BERETS
The Missions

by Pete Delmar

CAPSTONE PRESS
a capstone imprint

Velocity Books are published by Capstone Press,
1710 Roe Crest Drive, North Mankato, Minnesota 56003
www.capstonepub.com

Library of Congress Cataloging-in-Publication Data
Delmar, Pete.
The U.S. Army Green Berets : the missions / by Pete Delmar.
pages cm. —(Velocity. American special ops)
Includes bibliographical references and index.
Summary: "Describes the U.S. Army Green Berets, including their history, weapons, gear,
training, and missions"—Provided by publisher.
Audience: Ages 8-13.
ISBN 978-1-4765-0113-0 (library binding)
ISBN 978-1-4765-3587-6 (ebook PDF)
1. United States. Army. Special Forces—Juvenile literature. I. Title.
UA34.S64D45 2014
356'.1670973—dc23   2012045289

Editorial Credits
Carrie Braulick Sheely, editor; Bobbie Nuytten, designer; Kathy McColley, production specialist

Photo Credits
Alamy: military tanks vehicles guns, 37 (top), Stocktrek Images, Inc./Tom Weber, 39; AP Photo:
Laurnet Rebours, 14 (bottom), U.S. Army via Airborne & Special Operations Museum, 31;
Capstone Studio: Karon Dubke, 4 (left), 5 (both); Corbis: Bettmann, 19, 20, ZUMA Press/The
Orange County Register/Michael Goulding, 30; DoD photo, 43, Staff Sgt. Edward Braly, USAF, 6,
Tech. Sgt. Manuel J. Martinez, USAF, 10; Newscom: Warner Bros./Seven Arts, 4 (right), ZUMA
Press/Gary Kieffer, 27, ZUMA Press/Mi D. Seitelman, 7 (bottom); PEOSoldier, 35, 40 (bottom);
Shutterstock: Digital Storm, 13, 18, 37 (silhouettes), michal812, 8, Olinchuk, 14 (top), 42,
Pjasha, 21, RCPPHOTO, 41, Vartanov Anatoly, 40 (top); U.S. Air Force photo by Tech. Sgt. DeNoris
Mickle, 44 (top); U.S. Army Corps of Engineers photo, 17; U.S. Army photo, 7 (top), 16, 25, 45,
Master Sgt. Donald Sparks, cover, Sgt. Karl Williams, 38, Sgt. Vincent Byrd, 44 (bottom), Staff
Sgt. Marcus Butler, 32, Staff Sgt. Russell Klika, 28, Staff Sgt. Teddy Wade, 23, Sgt. David William
McLean, 22nd MPAD, 29; U.S. Navy photo by MC1 Miguel Angel Contreras, 36

Artistic Effects
Shutterstock

Quote Notes
Pg. 31 John F. Kennedy quotes from the John F. Kennedy
Presidential Library and Museum website.

Capstone Press thanks Ms. Jennifer Paquette, Executive Director of
the Green Beret Foundation, for reviewing this book for content accuracy.

Printed in the United States of America in
North Mankato, Minnesota.
102013   007731R

TABLE OF CONTENTS

POP CULTURE ICONS

On March 5, 1966, an unusual song hit the top spot on the *Billboard* pop music charts. It wasn't a typical bubbly pop tune celebrating the good times. Instead, it was a patriotic song about one of the world's top military forces.

The song was called "Ballad of the Green Berets." It brought a lot of public attention to the U.S. Army Special Forces, the official name for the Green Berets. The song's popularity led it to be used in many movie sound tracks. It has even been sung by movie characters.

Green Beret stories in every form have caught people's attention since the group formed in 1952. One well-known example is *The Green Berets*. Robin Moore wrote this book after witnessing events of the Vietnam War (1959–1975) firsthand. Although it is fiction, it is based on the war experiences of real Green Berets. The book was released in 1965 and quickly became a best-seller. In 1968 the book was made into a movie starring John Wayne, a huge movie star at the time. From 1983 to 1987, a TV series called *The A-Team* aired about the Green Berets.

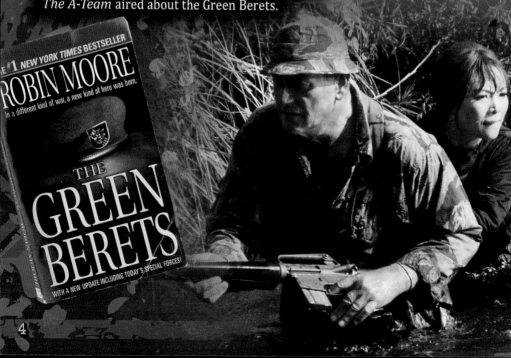

#1 NEW YORK TIMES BESTSELLER
ROBIN MOORE
In a different kind of war, a new kind of hero was born.

THE GREEN BERETS
WITH A NEW UPDATE INCLUDING TODAY'S SPECIAL FORCES!

The Green Berets' historic popularity shows the great respect that Americans have for the elite group. Green Berets have earned this respect by bringing skill and bravery to their dangerous missions.

More Examples of Green Berets in Pop Culture:

1987

The Green Beret G.I. Joe doll is released. Known as Lieutenant Falcon, he is dressed in jungle camouflage and a green beret. The doll also appears in G.I. Joe cartoons and comic books.

1982

Actor Sylvester Stallone stars as ex-Green Beret John Rambo in the movie *First Blood*. Stallone made three more Rambo movies. The last one came out in 2008.

2010

The movie *The A-Team* is released. The movie is based on the 1980s TV show.

THE **A-TEAM**

"THE BEST ACTION FILM IN YEARS!"

Fact

"Ballad of the Green Berets" was written and sung by Green Beret medic and Staff Sergeant Barry Sadler. It held its number one position on the *Billboard* pop music chart for five weeks. *Billboard* magazine rated it the number one hit for all of 1966.

pop music—a type of music that has its roots in rock 'n' roll but which is ever-changing in style; pop music is considered to be music that is the "most popular" with the greatest number of listeners

beret—a visorless wool cap with a tight headband and a flat top; members of the U.S. Army Special Forces are called Green Berets because of the berets they wear

Chapter 1

THE QUIET PROFESSIONALS

Although the Hollywood version of the Green Berets is glamorous, it doesn't truly reflect the real situation. Green Berets are known as the "quiet professionals" for good reason. Those who make it onto Army Special Forces teams have completed some of the toughest military training in the world. They are expert unconventional warriors. These soldiers take on the most dangerous and difficult military missions.

PRIMARY MISSIONS

COUNTERTERRORISM:
to prevent or respond to terrorism and train foreign military forces to fight terrorism

DIRECT ACTION:
to perform quick, surprise attacks; direct action missions are often done to seize enemy weapons or information. They are also done to rescue people or property from enemies.

FOREIGN INTERNAL DEFENSE:
to organize, assist, and train the militaries of foreign countries to better protect themselves; foreign internal defense missions are used to restore peace in foreign nations. They are also used during times of peace to prepare nations for enemy attacks.

SPECIAL RECONNAISSANCE:
to gather information on enemies in enemy territory; soldiers gather information about an enemy's movement, camps, and weapons.

COUNTER-PROLIFERATION:
to keep enemy nations from building up stockpiles of deadly weapons, especially weapons of mass destruction (WMDs)

INFORMATION OPERATIONS:
to gather information about enemy operations while keeping U.S. information safe from enemies

UNCONVENTIONAL WARFARE (UW):
to use non-ordinary methods of war and to train foreign forces or civilians in these methods; UW involves secretly gathering information and the use of guerilla warfare. This type of warfare uses small groups of fighters to carry out quick surprise attacks against enemy forces.

unconventional—a way of fighting that is not like ordinary hand-to-hand combat
terrorism—acts committed by people who use violence and fear to further their cause

Missions Around the World

From their beginning in 1952, Green Berets have trained to perform missions globally. Here are some places where Green Berets have conducted missions.

1989—Panama: invaded Panama to capture dictator Manuel Noriega and destroy his forces

1980s—El Salvador: trained El Salvadorans for combat to protect the nation from a rebellion

Late 1980s—Colombia: carried out counterterrorism and counter-drug missions

Fact

Women are currently not allowed to become Green Berets. They work for the Army Special Forces only in support roles based in the United States. However, in 2013 a ban keeping women from serving in military combat roles was lifted.

1990–1991 and 2003–2010—Iraq:
During Operation Desert Storm (1990–1991) and preparations for it, Green Berets operated in and around Iraq. They helped protect Saudi Arabia from Iraqi invasion and conducted reconnaissance missions. Years later, Special Forces soldiers conducted missions in Iraq during Operation Iraqi Freedom (2003–2010).

1970—North Vietnam:
During the Vietnam War, Army Special Forces soldiers attempted a rescue of American prisoners from a prison camp. However, the prisoners had been moved to a nearby camp before the soldiers' arrival.

1961—Laos:
protected Laos from communist rebels and later from communist North Vietnam

2001-present—Afghanistan:
carried out counterterrorism missions during Operation Enduring Freedom (2001–)

1992—Somalia, Africa:
provided security so that food supplies could be delivered to starving Somalians

In addition to their seven primary missions, the Green Berets' other missions include:
- counter-drug operations
- demolitions and bomb defusing
- combat search-and-rescue missions
- offensive raids
- peacekeeping missions

communist—a country or person practicing communism; communism is a political system in which there is no private property and everything is owned by the government

PART OF A LARGER GROUP

The Army Special Forces, or Green Berets, are part of a larger group of skilled unconventional warriors known as the Special Operations Forces (SOF). Because the names "special forces" and "special operations forces" are so similar, they can be confusing. The Army, Navy, Marines, and Air Force all have SOFs. All of the military's SOF members receive intense training and share many skills. However, each is focused on a certain specialty. The Army Special Forces, the Army Rangers, and the Navy SEALs are three of the most well-known SOFs.

U.S. Army Special Forces soldiers conduct a training exercise with a military working dog in 2011.

USSOCOM oversees the U.S. Army Special Operations Command as well as the special operations commands of the Navy, Marine Corps, and Air Force.

U.S. Air Force Special Operations Command

U.S. Navy Special Warfare Command

U.S. Special Operations Command USSOCOM

U.S. Marine Corps Forces Special Operations Command

U.S. Army Special Operations Command Fort Bragg, NC

U.S. Army Special Forces (Green Berets)

Support Groups: 4th Psychological Operations Group, 528th Sustainment Brigade, 95th Civil Affairs Brigade

75th Ranger Regiment

John F. Kennedy Special Warfare Center and School

160th Special Operations Aviation Regiment

The U.S. Army Special Operations Command oversees other groups in addition to the Green Berets.

INSIDE THE GREEN BERETS

The Army Special Forces includes five active groups. These groups are called Special Forces Groups (SFGs). Each SFG focuses on a certain geographical area called an Area of Responsibility (AOR). In addition to the five active SFGs, there are two Army National Guard SFGs. Soldiers in these SFGs are part-time soldiers.

Each SFG is also divided into smaller units called battalions. Most SFGs have four battalions. Usually at least one of an SFG's battalions is stationed at the U.S. command center, or base.

Group	Group Location
1st SFG AOR: Pacific	Fort Lewis, WA (3 battalions) Okinawa, Japan (1 battalion)
3rd SFG AOR: Sub-Saharan Africa	Fort Bragg, NC (4 battalions)
5th SFG AOR: Middle East, Central Asia	Fort Campbell, KY (4 battalions)
7th SFG AOR: Latin America, Caribbean	Eglin Air Force Base, FL (4 battalions)
10th SFG AOR: Europe, Northern Africa	Fort Carson, Colorado (3 battalions) Stuttgart, Germany (1 battalion)

A battalion has separate companies. Each company usually has six A-teams and a B-team. While A-teams generally conduct direct operations, the B-team provides support. A-teams are usually made up of 12 men:

commander
oversees all team action

assistant commander [warrant officer]
second in command

operations/intelligence sergeant
gathers information about enemies; makes and breaks secret codes

non-commissioned officer in charge [NCOIC]
oversees training and may be a leader in combat missions

weapons sergeants [2 members]
experts in operating and maintaining weapons

communications sergeants [2 members]
experts in using all communications devices

medical sergeants [2 members]
trained to treat injuries in the field

engineering sergeants [2 members]
experts in using and defusing explosives; trained to build and repair roads, bridges, buildings, and other structures

IN ACTION!

OPERATION DESERT SHIELD
Middle East, 1990

In 1990 Iraq invaded and seized control of its smaller Middle Eastern neighbor, Kuwait. The U.S. military responded in Kuwait's defense. This mission was known as Operation Desert Shield. Three battalions of the 5th Special Forces Group were sent to the region to find out exactly what was happening. The Middle East was the 5th SFG's Area of Responsibility. These Green Berets had a deep understanding of Middle Eastern culture, politics, and the Arabic language.

The 5th SFG's main mission was to gather information, or "ground truth," on the enemy. U.S. military leaders feared the Iraqis might also try to invade Saudi Arabia.

A U.S. soldier conducts searches in Kuwait City for remaining Iraqi soldiers during Operation Desert Storm.

Iraq

Kuwait

Saudi Arabia

OPERATION DESERT SHIELD AND DESERT STORM TIMELINE

August 2, 1990:
Iraqi president Saddam Hussein invades and seizes control of Kuwait.

August 7:
U.S. military commanders take action in response to the invasion.

October 13, 1990–February 10, 1991:
The 5th SFG operates along the borders and goes behind enemy lines in support of Saudi and Kuwaiti forces.

January 17, 1991:
U.S. forces determine that Iraqi forces are not going to pull out of Kuwait. The U.S. military ends Operation Desert Shield and engages in a war known as Operation Desert Storm, or the Gulf War.

February 17, 1991:
Kuwaiti troops free their capital, Kuwait City. The only American troops to accompany them in taking back the city are the men of the 5th SFG.

Much of what the Special Forces did during Operation Desert Shield has not been revealed. However, these are some of their reported activities:

- watched enemy movement along Iraq's borders and sent early warnings about Iraqi activity to U.S. command centers; Green Berets sometimes hid for days in specially built underground "spider holes."

- sent information to U.S. command centers on the locations of Iraqi scud missiles and other hidden targets

- patrolled Saudi-Kuwait border with Saudi special operations forces

- watched and reported build-up of Iraqi troops and weapons along the Iraqi-Kuwait border

- trained Kuwaiti soldiers in guerilla warfare, including combat search and rescue, special reconnaissance, defense tactics, and direct action missions; Green Berets also provided training on vehicle and equipment repair.

- collected soil samples to see how the Army's heavy tanks would hold up on desert sand

- rescued pilots whose aircraft had been shot down while defending against the Iraqi invasion

- cleared pathways through mine fields and trenches created by Iraqis so that regular U.S. troops could get through

Chapter 2

GREEN BERET HISTORY

The Army Special Forces was the U.S. military's first official special operations group. The group got its start in May 1952 at Fort Bragg, North Carolina. But it wasn't until the 1960s that these highly skilled troops became known as the Green Berets. When the force formed, it was officially known as the 10th Special Forces Group. The group included 10 men. The group's founder and commander was Colonel Aaron Bank. The unit also included one supporting officer and eight enlisted men. But in the next few months, word got out about the group. Soon hundreds of men began applying.

During World War II (1939-1945), Bank had been involved with the Army's Office of Strategic Services (OSS). The OSS was an intelligence gathering operation. Bank used his OSS experience to train his new 10th Special Forces Group. His original goal was to train the 10th SFG soldiers to work behind enemy lines. He wanted the SFG troops to stop Soviet soldiers if they moved to invade Europe.

Colonel Aaron Bank

Fort Bragg has been the headquarters of Army special operations soldiers since 1952. The huge base has many offices, houses, and training areas.

The soldiers graduated from their special forces basic training later in 1952. They then were given additional training. This second phase was a demanding course in individual and team skills. The men of the 10th SFG became experts in hand-to-hand combat, setting off explosives, and many other useful war techniques. With these varied skills, the soldiers were soon doing much more than what Bank first had in mind.

Fact

The 10th SFG was given its name to fool U.S. enemies into thinking nine other SFG groups were already active somewhere.

EARLY GREEN BERET MISSIONS

In September 1953 members of the 10th SFG took on an unexpected mission. Half of the group was sent to Germany. Protests had recently been held against the communist East German government in the city of Berlin. The United States had been enemies of Germany in World War II. The U.S. military wanted to create a presence in Germany in case war broke out. If it did, the United States would already have forces behind enemy lines. The other half of the 10th SFG remained in Fort Bragg and became known as the 77th SFG.

From Germany the 10th SFG went on to Korea. During the Korean War (1950-1953), the group went behind enemy lines in North Korea. Communist North Korea had invaded South Korea. North Korea wanted to force South Korea into becoming communist.

The United States wanted to stop the spread of communism. Green Berets worked in support of South Korean troops.

Fact
Today the 77th SFG is known as the 7th SFG.

Green Berets train Montagnard tribesmen in
South Vietnam during the Vietnam War.

In the late 1950s and early 1960s, Special
Forces teams were secretly sent to Laos and later
to Vietnam. In both places the Green Berets taught
combat tactics to villagers and small native militias.
The United States wanted to help the natives
fight the North Vietnamese and other communist
and anti-democratic groups.

When North Vietnam invaded South Vietnam to start
the Vietnam War, Green Berets continued to train the
South Vietnamese. The Green Berets also led combat
missions deep in enemy territory. In all, Army Special
Forces soldiers spent 14 years in Vietnam, where their
outstanding service was widely recognized.

militia—a group of volunteer citizens organized to fight, but
who are not professional soldiers

IN ACTION!

OPERATION WHITE STAR
Laos, 1959-1962

BACKGROUND: Laotians were being threatened by communists who wanted to take over Laos. These communists were supported by North Vietnam, a nearby communist country. The French military was giving monetary aid to the Laotians and conducting combat training. But the arrival of the Green Berets brought new life to Laos' fight to stay a free nation.

MISSION: The Green Berets were sent to advise and to provide equipment, training, and military support to the Laotian government. Later the Green Berets were sent to train villagers in guerilla warfare. It was one of the earliest Green Beret missions of foreign internal defense.

After the Vietnam War started, U.S. soldiers continued to patrol the Laos-South Vietnam border.

Timeline of Events

JULY 1959

The operation begins under the name Operation Hotfoot. Special Forces soldiers from the 77th SFG arrive in Laos. They wear civilian clothing to avoid calling attention to themselves. Later they begin wearing military clothing.

JULY-AUGUST 1959

Commander Lieutenant Colonel Arthur D. "Bull" Simons sets up mobile training teams (MTTs) in five military districts defined by the Royal Laotian Army.

SEPTEMBER 1, 1959

The MTTs begin training a class of 1,138 Laotians.

NOVEMBER 1959

A sixth MTT is added. The teams begin training Laotian villagers in companies of 100 men.

JANUARY 1960

The Kau hill tribe excels under the supervision of the Green Berets. Army Special Forces teams begin to rotate in and out of Laos.

DECEMBER 17, 1960

Laos' French military advisors and combat instructors leave the country.

APRIL 1961

Operation Hotfoot changes its name to Operation White Star as a new Green Beret unit rotates into Laos.

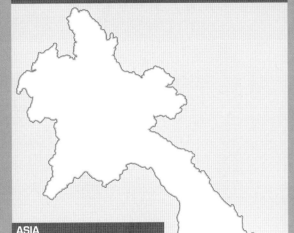

LAOS

ASIA

OCEANIA

1961 TO JULY 1962

The number of Green Berets on the White Star mission gradually increases to 433 men.

JULY 23, 1962

Laos successfully declares itself a **neutral** country, officially ending Operation White Star.

OCTOBER 1962

The last White Star troops leave Laos as the focus of war turns to Vietnam. There, the experience gained working with the Laotians serves the Green Berets well.

neutral—not taking any side in a war

Chapter 3

BECOMING A GREEN BERET

Like the first Army Special Forces soldiers, all Green Beret candidates are volunteers. In earlier days, these volunteers were sent to train in a filthy swamp as soon as they arrived in Fort Bragg. Later, Army officials decided this practice wasn't respectful of the men who had come there willingly. They removed this training step.

But joining the ranks of the Green Berets still is not easy. Special Forces training is comprehensive. It takes a long time to complete, and it is very physically demanding. It also has a more academic focus than other U.S. military SOF training programs. In particular, the Green Berets take extended occupational and foreign language training.

Fact

Less than one-fourth of the men who start Army Special Forces training make it through every phase to become a Special Forces team member.

At every stage of the process, the demands get more difficult. With each phase, more candidates drop out or are disqualified because they can't meet the requirements. In the end, the most capable applicants stand alone. These soldiers are qualified to wear the green beret.

academic—form of schooling in which students learn information rather than hands-on skills

Before a Green Beret candidate even gets to the training stage, he has to meet several requirements, including:

- be male
- be 20 to 30 years old
- be a U.S. citizen
- have a high school diploma
- have 20/20 vision or vision correctable to 20/20
- pass many difficult physical and mental tests
- qualify and volunteer for airborne training
- qualify for a secret security clearance

TOUGH TRAINING

Anyone who meets all the basic entrance requirements might feel lucky. But every Special Forces candidate faces grueling training. Here are the training stages he must complete to become a Green Beret.

STAGE 1 — SPECIAL OPS PREP COURSE

The Special Operations Preparation Course (SOPC) is the first step in the journey. It is sometimes known as the pre-SFAS.

WHERE IT HAPPENS: Fort Bragg, North Carolina

LENGTH: 30 days

PURPOSE: to help candidates prepare for the Special Forces Assessment and Selection (SFAS) course and the Special Forces Qualification Course (SFQC)

WHAT'S INVOLVED: a focus on physical training; a great deal of time is also spent on land navigation training.

Fact

No Special Forces candidates are allowed to give up until after the first week. Army officials believe that candidates are more likely to continue training if they can make it through one week.

During this course, those who pass the SOPC find out if they can handle being pushed to their breaking points. At this time, the men officially become Special Forces candidates. Over more than three punishing weeks, potential Green Berets test their physical and mental skills. The three-part SFAS is considered phase one of the "real" Special Forces training.

WHERE IT HAPPENS: Camp Mackall, North Carolina

LENGTH: 24 days

PURPOSE: to test a candidate's survival skills; to determine how quick, athletic, resourceful, and intelligent he is

WHAT'S INVOLVED: three parts that test physical, emotional, and mental capabilities

navigation—following a course point by point to get from one place to another

STAGE 2 (SFAS)

PART 1

The first part of the SFAS focuses on physical and psychological testing.
  Tough tasks include:
  - swimming 164 feet (50 meters) in full gear and boots
  - marching 150 miles (241 km) carrying a weapon and a 50-pound (23-kilogram) backpack
  - carrying two sand-filled duffel bags 6.2 miles (10 km) (The sandbags are meant to be similar in weight to human bodies.)

PART 2

Part two brings more challenging physical endurance tests.
  Tough tasks include:
  - completing a 1.5-mile (2.4-km) obstacle course with numerous vertical obstacles such as fences and walls
  - completing a land navigation course carrying a fully loaded pack

Fact

Army trainers and commanding officers look for men who can both pull their own weight and look out for their fellow recruits. Experience has shown that those who continually put their own welfare before that of others don't make good Special Forces soldiers.

PART 3

In part three, soldiers are evaluated on teamwork skills and leadership abilities. Recruits are divided into 12-man teams. The teams are put in stressful situations to see how members react, work together, and solve problems. For each assignment, the team gets a mission statement and some necessary equipment to complete the task.

Tough tasks include:
- figuring out how to haul a huge, heavy trailer over 12 miles (19 km)
- planning and constructing a large building or other structure

More men quit or fail to pass at each part. At the end of SFAS, only about half of the candidates will qualify to go on to the next phase, the Special Forces Qualification Course (SFQC).

SPECIAL FORCES QUALIFICATION COURSE (SFQC)—"Q COURSE"

The SFQC is widely known as the Q course. It is divided into six separate phases. This is where the testing becomes tougher than ever. Those who successfully complete the Q course become Green Berets.

WHERE IT HAPPENS: Fort Bragg, North Carolina

LENGTH: from six months to 1 year

WHAT'S INVOLVED: testing of both physical and mental capabilities

1 COURSE ORIENTATION AND HISTORY

This training phase introduces candidates to how the Special Forces operate. Candidates learn about the group's history and its culture. They also take a wellness screening and assessment.

2 LANGUAGE AND CULTURE TRAINING

Every Green Beret in training must be fluent in at least one language besides English. Which language they learn usually determines where the successful candidates will be stationed. Some of the main languages trainees learn are Arabic, Chinese, Russian, and Spanish.

tactical combat skills training during Q Course

SMALL UNIT TACTICS (SUT)

3 Small Unit Tactics training includes live-fire exercises, urban warfare training, and training to contain attempts to overthrow governments. This phase also includes Survival, Evasion, Resistance, and Escape (SERE) training. SERE training teaches candidates how to escape if they are captured by enemies and how to survive in enemy territory.

MOS TRAINING

4 Military occupational specialties (MOS) are assigned based on a volunteer's interest, natural abilities, and background. MOS training is provided for jobs as a medical specialist, weapons specialist, communication specialist, and officer.

UW CULEX (ROBIN SAGE COURSE)

5 During this segment, soldiers come together to learn Special Forces organization and standard ways of operating. They also begin training in specific Special Forces missions—unconventional warfare, direct action missions, and various airborne operations.

GRADUATION

6 The graduation phase lasts one week. Candidates are awarded their green berets and Special Forces tabs. A tab identifies a soldier as a member of Army Special Forces. It is worn on a soldier's uniform. Soldiers are allowed to wear their tabs throughout their military careers. In this phase, soldiers are also introduced to their teams.

student of the Special Forces Sniper Course

Success in the Q course means a soldier has made it into the Green Berets. But further training opportunities are available, such as courses in advanced parachute training and **sniper** training. These courses aren't required, but a Green Beret can select any further training he is interested in.

fluent—able to easily speak a language
evasion—a sneaky way of avoiding or escaping an attack
sniper—a soldier trained to shoot at long-distance targets from a hidden place

Chapter 4

READY, ARMED, AND EQUIPPED

No matter what Green Berets are doing, they always dress the part and come prepared. When not in combat, they wear their non-combat uniforms. When in combat, they are dressed in protective gear from head to toe. They use the best weapons and gear for their jobs.

The Green Beret

When not in combat, nothing identifies a soldier as a member of Army Special Forces more than his headgear. The Green Beret hat is generally worn everywhere except in combat.

all-wool beret in hunter green

A soldier's **flash** is worn on the front left side of the beret. This red flash represents the 7th SFG.

The Green Beret **crest** is also worn on the front left side of the beret on top of the flash.

Timeline of the Famous Green Beret

Early 1950s

Army Special Forces troops in North Carolina start wearing green berets, even though it's not an authorized part of their uniform.

1955

Following the trend in the United States, an Army Special Forces unit stationed in Germany starts wearing green berets.

1957

The Army orders Special Forces soldiers to stop wearing green berets. However, overseas troops who are not under the Army's watchful eye continue to wear them.

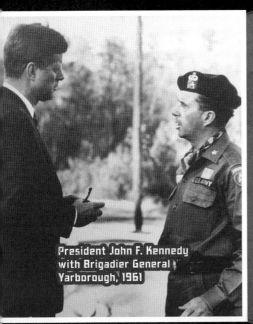

President John F. Kennedy with Brigadier General Yarborough, 1961

1961

President John F. Kennedy plans to visit Fort Bragg to see Special Forces soldiers demonstrate their skills. He makes a special request that the soldiers all wear green berets. Special Forces soldiers scramble, trying to borrow and dye berets to go with their uniforms.

Shortly after his visit, President Kennedy officially approves the green beret as part of the Special Forces uniform. He writes to commanding officer Brigadier General William P. Yarborough, "I know that you and the members of your command will carry on ... in a manner which is both worthy and inspiring. I am sure that the green beret will be a mark of distinction in the trying times ahead."

April 11, 1962

President Kennedy sends an important memo to the U.S. Army, writing, "The green beret is again becoming a symbol of excellence, a badge of courage, a mark of distinction in the fight for freedom."

flash—a U-shaped woven patch with a color and design that shows which Special Forces group a soldier belongs to

crest—an ornament worn on a uniform to symbolize or identify one's role or position in the military

The Army's noncombat uniforms are traditionally green. The Army began issuing dark blue uniforms in 2010. As of 2014 all Army personnel will be required to wear the blue uniforms.

uniform includes:

- blue coat and trousers
- white short- or long-sleeved shirt
- black tie

A Special Forces soldier stands behind a wreath shaped like a green beret. The wreath was used in a wreath-laying ceremony at President Kennedy's grave site in 2012.

U.S. ARMY SPECIAL FORCES

Fact

A blue Army uniform was first worn by soldiers in the Continental army of 1779.

A Green Beret's uniform might display a number of badges, crests, or other decorations. Each has a special meaning. Many of these signify a soldier's rank, skills, or other information about his Army role. They may show the wearer's occupational specialties. For example, the Army Special Forces Desert patch is worn by Green Berets who have been on desert missions. A High Altitude Low Opening (HALO) wings tab shows that a Green Beret is an accomplished HALO parachute specialist. Until July 1997 only Special Forces soldiers could wear this badge. Today any military HALO expert can wear one.

HONORING PRESIDENT KENNEDY

On November 22, 1988, people from around the world came to Arlington Cemetery in Virginia for an important memorial service. It was the 25th anniversary of the death of President Kennedy. The visitors gathered at the president's grave site. For the service, an unusual wreath was placed on Kennedy's grave. It was shaped like a green beret.

The wreath had this shape for a historical reason. Shortly after Kennedy's death, Army Special Forces soldiers were assigned to guard his grave. At the funeral in November 1963, a sergeant in charge of these men placed his green beret on Kennedy's coffin out of respect. This powerful gesture was the basis for the wreath placed on his grave 25 years later. The U.S. Army Special Forces has continued holding wreath-laying ceremonies at Kennedy's grave site to honor him and his commitment to the unit.

COMBAT READY!

A soldier's attire and equipment in the field depends on the region, weather conditions, or tasks to be done. Here are a few standard items a Green Beret might wear on the job in places like Afghanistan.

MULTICAM JACKET AND TROUSERS:
MultiCam is a seven-color, multi-environment camouflage pattern.

HYDRATION POUCH:
supplies easy-to-carry drinking water and allows soldiers to drink hands-free. Soldiers bite down on a valve and the water flows through the hose.

ARMY ADVANCED COMBAT HELMET:
This lightweight helmet provides protection from bullets. The helmet can be equipped with communication gear and night-vision devices. It may have a MultiCam cover on it.

TACTICAL ASSAULT PANEL [TAP]:
worn against the chest for carrying ammunition and other gear. The TAP can be used by itself or mounted on a vest.

KNEEPADS

HEAVY-DUTY BOOTS

SUNGLASSES OR TINTED GOGGLES

GLOVES:
offer short-term protection from temperatures of up to 800 degrees Fahrenheit (427 degrees Celsius)

TOUGH EQUIPMENT

In late 2001 some members of the 5th SFG were conducting counterterrorism missions in Afghanistan. Their mission required them to travel to a location in Afghanistan that could only be reached on horseback. But these tough men, who later became known as "horse soldiers," couldn't handle the typical Afghani wooden saddles. They asked for western-style leather ones to be shipped in.

VEHICLES

Special Forces troops rely on several vehicles to help them complete their dangerous missions.

Land Vehicles

HMMWV (Humvee)

HMMWV stands for High Mobility Multipurpose Wheeled Vehicle. But these useful vehicles are more commonly known as Humvees. The large armored vehicles are lightweight but tough. Four-wheel drive allows them to operate in rough terrain. Depending on the need, they can be outfitted to carry people, weapons, or equipment. Some are equipped as ambulances.

PRACTICAL CONSIDERATIONS:

A single Humvee may carry a great deal of equipment. Reducing vehicle weight can be an important consideration. The vehicle's weight is reduced by stripping off the doors and making cuts in the bulletproof roof.

MAIN PURPOSE:

transporting troops into and out of mission areas

Kawasaki KLR250 Motorcycle

Each A-team gets two slightly modified Kawasaki KLR250 motorcycles. These dirt bikes have powerful engines and knobby tires. Soldiers can easily ride them fast on rough terrain.

MAIN PURPOSE:
getting quickly to locations that would be harder and slower for larger vehicles to travel to; scouting missions before larger groups of forces move in

Water Vehicles

Rigid Hull Inflatable Boat (RHIB)

The Rigid Hull Inflatable Boat has a tough fiberglass hull, yet it is very lightweight. Most RHIBs are between 13 and 30 feet (4 and 9.1 m) long. The high-speed boats can travel about 52 miles (84 km) per hour.

MAIN PURPOSE:

to allow Special Forces units to perform ground reconnaissance of enemy territory; troop pick-up and drop-off at enemy beaches

ADVANTAGES:

lightweight, quiet, and speedy; can be used in launches from helicopters; able to handle the weight of a team in full gear as well as a mounted machine gun; able to withstand high winds and large waves

soldiers train with an RHIB

Kayaks

Special Forces kayaks are designed to be stealthy. They can move in complete silence at 5 miles (8 km) per hour. Two men travel in each kayak. In total, each kayak can carry 900 pounds (408 kg). On land, a folded-up kayak becomes an 88-pound (40-kg) piece of gear carried by one soldier.

Other special operations groups, such as the Navy SEALs, also use kayaks on their missions.

ADVANTAGES:
very stealthy; can be taken apart in five minutes

MAIN PURPOSE:
surprise enemy attacks

Fact

A 36-foot (11-m) RHIB can stay afloat in waves up to 46 feet (14 m) high.

WEAPONS

Army Special Forces use several different types of firearms. But these are their two main weapons.

BERETTA M9 PISTOL

The Beretta M9 is a semi-automatic handgun. Each time a bullet is fired, another one automatically slides into the empty chamber.

MAIN PURPOSE:
close combat

SPECIAL EQUIPMENT:
includes an Integrated Laser/White Light Pointer (ILWLP) to help soldiers aim

THE ILWLP IN ACTION

The battery-operated ILWLP is basically a high-tech flashlight attached to the M9 pistol. It can sight targets as well in the dark as it can in daylight. When using night-vision goggles, a soldier can get even better visibility.

M-4 CARBINE RIFLE

The lightweight M-4 Carbine is easy to take on long-distance trips. The M-4 is well known for its power and accuracy. It can hit targets up to 1,640 feet (500 m) away. The M-4 is used by other military special operations as well, including the Navy SEALs.

MAIN PURPOSE:
to reach targets at an extended range in close-quarters combat

ADVANTAGES:
customizable with other gear, including night-vision and laser sighting devices, a special handgrip, and a grenade launcher

DRAWBACK:
can jam if sand or other materials get into the parts

Fact

At Fort Bragg's Virtual Live Fire training facility, Special Forces soldiers fire the M-4 at images of "enemies" projected onto screens.

grenade—a small bomb that can be thrown or launched from a weapon

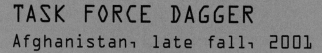
IN ACTION!

TASK FORCE DAGGER
Afghanistan, late fall, 2001

BACKGROUND: Task Force Dagger was the name of one of several joint special operations task forces. The U.S. military formed these task forces to carry out dangerous missions at the start of Operation Enduring Freedom (2001-) in Afghanistan.

CORE GROUP: a 12-man A-Team from the 5th SFG with backup from two other special operations groups from the Army and Air Force

MISSION: The main mission was to aid Afghan leaders and rebels in their fight against the Taliban and to hunt for members of the terrorist group al-Qaida. The 5th SFG and the Afghani commanders wanted to take control of several Taliban-ruled cities in the northern part of the country.

MISSION BASE CAMP: K2, a former Soviet airbase in southern Uzbekistan

DANGERS: The team had to fly into Afghanistan with winter coming. The harsh Afghan climate, with its mountain snowstorms and high winds, made traveling by roads almost impossible. But flying was dangerous too. In early October, the 5th SFG flew by helicopter into northern Afghanistan at night. The Air Force pilots had to navigate in the dark through heavy clouds, rain, and sandstorms. They were flying through narrow passages in mountains 16,000 feet (4,877 m) high. At some points they had to avoid enemy fire from the ground.

5th SFG Mission Steps

1. began moving into Panshir Valley in the fall of 2001

2. joined forces with a U.S. Central Intelligence Agency (CIA) team and Northern Alliance troops under command of Afghani warlord Fahim Khan

3. oversaw air strikes against Taliban-held locations in the Shomali Plain

4. As Taliban forces fled, Task Force Dagger members ordered further air strikes, freeing Bagram Air Base.

5. On November 14, Task Force Dagger troops and their Afghani allies freed Afghanistan's capital, Kabul, from enemy forces.

Early action by Task Force Dagger forces made a huge difference in the course of the mission. Many of al-Qaida's best trained and most experienced leaders were captured or killed.

U.S. special operations forces ride with Northern Alliance members on November 12, 2001.

Taliban—a radical group that was controlling much of Afghanistan in the late 1990s and early 2001; the U.S. military helped push the Taliban from power in late 2001

GEAR

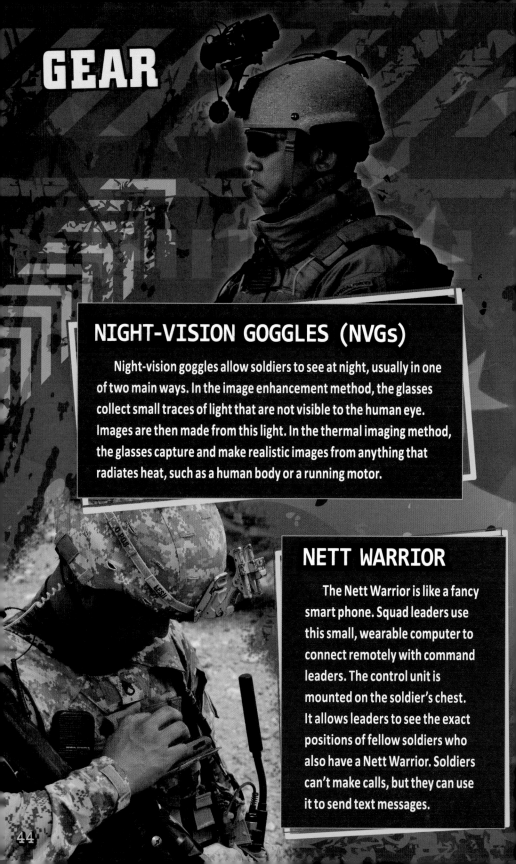

NIGHT-VISION GOGGLES (NVGs)

Night-vision goggles allow soldiers to see at night, usually in one of two main ways. In the image enhancement method, the glasses collect small traces of light that are not visible to the human eye. Images are then made from this light. In the thermal imaging method, the glasses capture and make realistic images from anything that radiates heat, such as a human body or a running motor.

NETT WARRIOR

The Nett Warrior is like a fancy smart phone. Squad leaders use this small, wearable computer to connect remotely with command leaders. The control unit is mounted on the soldier's chest. It allows leaders to see the exact positions of fellow soldiers who also have a Nett Warrior. Soldiers can't make calls, but they can use it to send text messages.

BRONZE BRUCE

A striking sculpture stands outside the Army Special Operations Command headquarters in Fort Bragg, North Carolina. It's a 12-foot (3.6-m) statue of a Green Beret soldier standing on a granite base. This memorial is known as "Bronze Bruce." Bruce is dedicated to all of the U.S. Army's special operations forces.

Green Berets are always on the job and their missions take them throughout the world. Wherever they are, they carry on a long tradition of courage and sacrifice.

GLOSSARY

academic (ak-uh-DEM-ik)—form of schooling in which students learn information rather than hands-on skills

beret (BUH-ray)—a visorless wool cap with a tight headband and a flat top

communist (KAHM-yuh-nist)—country or person practicing communism; communism is a political system in which there is no private property and everything is owned by the government

crest (KREST)—an ornament worn on a uniform to symbolize or identify one's role or position in the military

evasion (i-VAY-shuhn)—a sneaky way of avoiding or escaping an attack

flash (FLASH)—a U-shaped woven patch whose color and design show which SFG a soldier belongs to

fluent (FLOO-uhnt)—able to easily speak a language

grenade (gruh-NAYD)—a small bomb that can be thrown or launched

militia (muh-LISH-uh)—a group of volunteer citizens who serve as soldiers in emergencies

navigation (NAV-uh-gay-shun)—following a course point by point to get from one place to another

neutral (NOO-truhl)—not taking any side in a war

pop music (POP MYOO-zik)—type of music that has its roots in rock 'n' roll but which is ever-changing in style; pop music is considered to be music that is the "most popular" with the greatest number of listeners

reconnaissance (ree-KAH-nuh-suhnss)—a mission to gather information about an enemy

sniper (SNY-pur)—a soldier trained to shoot at long-distance targets

Taliban (TAL-i-ban)—a radical group that was controlling much of Afghanistan in the late 1990s and early 2001; the U.S. military helped push the Taliban from power in late 2001

terrorism (TER-ur-i-zuhm)—acts committed by people who use violence and fear to further their cause

unconventional (uhn-kin-VEN-shun-uhl)—a way of fighting that is not like ordinary hand-to-hand combat

READ MORE

Doeden, Matt. *Can You Survive the Special Forces?: An Interactive Survival Adventure*. You Choose: Survival. Mankato, Minn.: Capstone Press, 2013.

Hamilton, John. *United States Green Berets*. United States Armed Forces. Edina, Minn.: ABDO, 2012.

Nelson, Drew. *Green Berets*. U.S. Special Forces. New York: Gareth Stevens Pub., 2012.

INTERNET SITES

FactHound offers a safe, fun way to find Internet sites related to this book. All of the sites on FactHound have been researched by our staff.

Here's all you do:

Visit www.facthound.com

Type in this code: 9781476501130

www.FactHound.com

INDEX